Happy Father's Day
'2009

God Bless you
in his loving arms)
Love
& Prayers
Winston & Cynthia

SOUL SANCTUARY

*Images of the
African American
Worship Experience*

Jason Miccolo Johnson

Foreword by Gordon Parks · Introduction by Dr. Cain Hope Felder
Essays by Barbranda Lumpkins Walls, Rev. Cardes H. Brown, Jr., and
Rev. Dr. Lawrence N. Jones · Afterword by Bishop John Hurst Adams
Epilogue by Rev. Dr. H. Beecher Hicks, Jr.

BULFINCH PRESS
New York Boston

This book is dedicated to the memory of Dr. Joseph C. McKinney,
former treasurer of the AME Church.
Also, to Rev. Donald E. Robinson, founder and president of
Beacon House in Washington, D.C., a caring place where
young people's minds and hearts are being nurtured daily.
—Jason Miccolo Johnson

CONTENTS

KEY TO ABBREVIATIONS:
AME: African Methodist Episcopal; AMEZ: African Methodist Episcopal Zion;
CME: Christian Methodist Episcopal; COGIC: Church of God in Christ;
MBC: Missionary Baptist Church; SDA: Seventh-day Adventist

Richard Brockington grips a Bible as he listens attentively to the minister
on Palm Sunday at Ward Memorial AME Church, Washington, D.C., 1999

FOREWORD

Gordon Parks

Like multitudes of other black youths, Jason Miccolo Johnson has obviously lived through those emotional and religious rituals that lent shape not only to his life but to the larger black experience as well. Now, through the devout eye of his camera, he recaptures past moments of sacred worship. And he chooses to call the magnificent collection *Soul Sanctuary*.

How splendidly it awakens memories of those sacred Sundays of my own childhood, when God took over and all angels were black and sinners caught the wrath of a belligerent preacher's tongue. And not to be forgotten were the down-trodden and the faithful. Then, of course, there were the dispossessed.

Jason Johnson's efforts are thorough. His camera has taken intimate glimpses of just about everyone who worshipped in black churches wherever he found them. Missouri's Boot Heel country offered the stirring religion of the Pentecostal. Later, he watched black hands baptize Mt. Zion skulls in Memphis, Tennessee.

As a boy back in Kansas, I, too, watched those same baptisms, but to the uplift-ing sound of a black Methodist choir. The experiences were, without doubt, the same. Worshipping the Lord within the sanctuary of a black church is an experi-ence that's not to be surpassed. Jason's photographs pushed me back into that sanctuary, put Gabriel's horn in my hands, and urged me to shout, "Hallelujah!"

ABOVE: The historic Brown Chapel AME Church, which was the starting point of the 1965 Selma-to-Montgomery Voting Rights March, Selma, Alabama, 1996

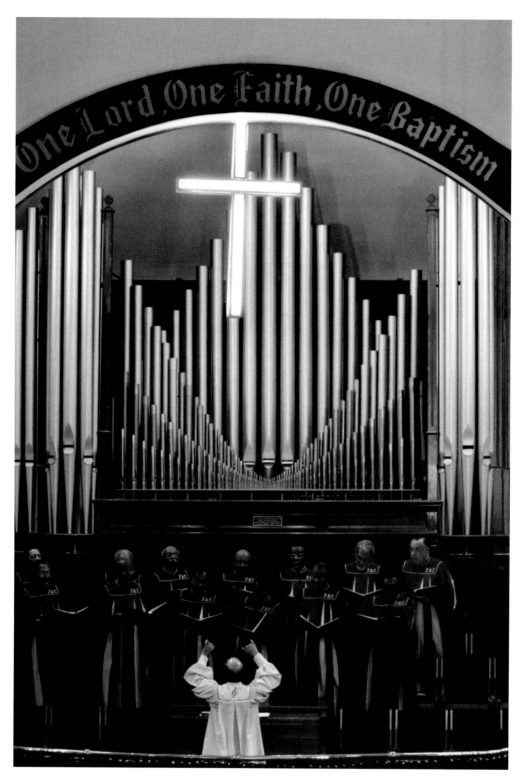

The Men's Choir of First Baptist Church, Norfolk, Virginia, 2005

PREFACE

Jason Miccolo Johnson

For as long as I can remember, the black church has held a quiet and strong grip upon my imagination. It was at Mt. Zion Missionary Baptist Church in Memphis, Tennessee—with great apprehension—that I clicked my first photo of a worship service, shooting from the balcony with a rangefinder camera.

My goal over the last ten years has been to capture for *Soul Sanctuary* many of those familiar images that I remember so vividly as a youth at Mt. Zion. The baptismal pool, the Sunday school classes held in the sanctuary, the sparkling shoes worn by the men, and the lovely and inventive hats worn by the church ladies. I can still remember the "old Mt. Zion" and the sight of feet rising and falling to the hardwood floor like pistons. The two-four beat of hands opening and closing in unison like human cymbals against the background of "Going up Yonder" or "Peace Be Still." Now, as in many churches I visited, those sights and sounds have been replaced with electronic instruments and the muffled timbre of feet pressing carpeting.

To me, the sanctuary is the soul of the black church, and the soul is the sanctuary of our spiritual being. Church was and is a paradise of "visualosity"—visual curiosity for the mind's eye. And Sundays in my family meant going to church.

One thing that stands out most in my mind about Sundays, before the spirit-filled singing, before the thunderous preaching, and before Sunday school, is how it

ABOVE: Brother James Littles reads his Bible
at Olivet MBC, Houston, Texas, 2005

9

always seemed to begin—the image of my aunt Mattie making biscuits to accompany bacon, eggs, and grits. Just by inhaling, I immediately knew what day of the week it was. She only made biscuits on Sunday mornings. Food for the soul, much like the preached word.

It has never been truer that "a picture is worth a thousand words" than in the case of the arresting and inspiring images found within the African American worship experience: allegorical images of struggle on the faces of saints and sinners alike; tears that flow triumphantly out of wells of joy and pain from internal demons still housed in the basements of our individual memories. *Soul Sanctuary* is my visual anthem to those who have persevered and found solace and strength within the black Christian church: the dedicated, the downtrodden, the dispossessed, and the faithful. Regardless of denomination or size, whether in a converted theater or a small storefront church, it's what happens inside the building when two or more are gathered together to hold service that I find most important.

Mrs. Mattie B. Stewart making biscuits from scratch on Sunday morning, Memphis, Tennessee, 1997

I think of *Soul Sanctuary* as a family photo album of familiar faces in familiar places that recall warm memories of my childhood. The emotional warmth and security that come from being part of a church family that loves you *for you* is some of what I looked for in my documentation of black folk worshipping. You might think of *Soul Sanctuary* as a day in the life of the black church—from the reverence of Saturday as the Sabbath among Seventh-day Adventists, on through a full day of Sunday services at black churches small and large in twenty states across America.

Ten years and fifteen thousand images ago, this photographic odyssey started in Memphis and has taken me from historic churches in New York City to megachurches in Dallas, and from the dusty back roads of the Mississippi Delta to the sun-drenched freeways of California.

The daily and weekly dynamics in the life of a church are particularly fascinating, but the Sunday rituals and rhythms that take place in small and large black sanctuaries of every denomination across America are nothing short of mesmerizing. I have seen the fading of old traditions and the introduction of new ones. Throughout my journey I've been shown nothing but amazing kindness. I have been fed in New Orleans, sheltered in Miami, driven around in St. Louis, and prayed over in Houston. And for that I feel truly blessed.

I recall the first major road trip for the book, for which I shut down my business for the month of November in 1997 in order to drive through every state east of the Mississippi River and south of Tennessee. Without having any particular church destination in mind, I allowed myself to be led by the spirit. From Memphis I drove south through Mississippi, making friends and meeting some relatives for the first time.

By the time I reached Greenville, Mississippi, I had the formula down pat for finding the black community. First find natural and man-made boundaries—such as bodies of water, bridges, railroads, and expressways. The black community is most likely just on the other side. Failing that, I'd look for Martin Luther King, Jr., Street, Avenue, or Boulevard, which almost always goes through a black neighborhood.

To find out about the various churches in town, I sought the best soul food restaurant or beauty salon and inquired inside. Most black folk I met were more than happy to tell me about *their* church. From that bit of oral research, I was now blessed with the names of several churches and ministers to contact. On Sundays, I would often visit up to three churches per city, capturing as many images as possible after explaining my project to the pastor and getting his or her permission to photograph their church.

Stewardess Ellen White prepares to pray at Ward Memorial AME Church, Washington, D.C., 1999

Once I was inside a church, the true challenge of the project really began. There was always the difficulty of shooting only in the available light, since I wanted to avoid the intrusion of flash or lighting equipment. This often meant finding creative ways to capture the actions and reactions of the subjects and the spirit of the environment in low-light situations. I also had to learn how to render pleasing darker skin tones in white uniforms while holding the details of both. Along the way I documented highly animated preachers, dedicated deacons and stewardesses, rhythmic choirs, passionate praise dancers, and the wide range of emotions from solemn to ecstatic found within a congregation at any given moment.

Throughout *Soul Sanctuary*, which follows the chronological format of a typical church bulletin, I've tried to tell you what I've seen and show you what I've felt, using a visual "call-and-response" style of shooting. *Soul Sanctuary* is about witnessing the story of the African American worship experience through focusing on the subjects' hands and eyes, one of my photographic trademarks. If the eyes are the windows to the soul, then truly the hands are the tour guides. Every soul deserves a good sanctuary—a *Soul Sanctuary*.

Dr. Jacquelyn Grant prays that her words might be blessed before delivering the morning sermon on Annual Women's Day at Allen Temple Baptist Church, Oakland, California, 1998

INTRODUCTION
Dr. Cain Hope Felder

*E*ach week across this country, a sacred tradition continues to take place in count‑ less communities—urban, suburban, and rural. It is a tradition born in the brush arbors of slave days long gone and yet revitalized Sunday after Sunday for mil‑ lions of African Americans. I refer to the core element of African American spiri‑ tuality, the black church worship service. This "soulful spirituality" is reflected in the many different textures and hues of fervent prayer, songs of joy, sorrow, and paradoxical triumph, at times punctuated with a "holy dance" culminating in the preached word, followed closely by a benediction.

Perhaps more significant than any other cultural expression among African Americans, far outdistancing jazz or rap, athletics or the arts, is the soulful worship service collectively perpetuated each week in the black church.

All of us owe a great debt to the spiritual eye of Jason Miccolo Johnson for this extraordinary offering of fine photographic artistry found in *Soul Sanctuary: Images of the African American Worship Experience*. Throughout this volume, the author's deep affection for and appreciation of the black church is consistently evident as he deftly documents for posterity candid and dramatic seminal pictures of black folk at worship, despite the challenge of using only existing available light. In some cases he freezes motion, in others, shows the blur of movement.

ABOVE: A family of four departs early morning
services at Bethel MBC, Tallahassee, Florida, 2005

This book is a visual collector's item. It is the first comprehensive photography book that shows so beautifully African Americans of various denominations at worship. Johnson has managed to precisely capture each of these glorified postures with his trademark attention paid to the subject's eyes and hands.

Having traveled to twenty states and visited more than 200 African American churches over the past decade, Jason Miccolo Johnson has applied the skills of his craft to provide not just African Americans but everyone, regardless of race, ethnicity, or denomination, with this wonderful gift from the black church worship experience. Indeed, *Soul Sanctuary* offers insights that might be particularly instructive for those who are not African American and may have never set foot in a black church, or for those who are only acquainted with the black church through the popular stereotypes of American public media.

Sister Johnnie Jeffries shakes her tambourine during Easter service at Temple of Deliverance COGIC, Memphis, Tennessee, 2005

Each of the six chapters of *Soul Sanctuary* opens with an essay that provides a helpful interpretive framework for the rich assortment of photographs that Jason Miccolo Johnson has selected for that segment of the book. Together, these essays and photographs illuminate the heightened leadership role of the laity in general, and women in particular, within today's black church. Readers also can see some of the ways in which the black church in recent years has taken advantage of more sophisticated forms of technology to enhance the worship experience through sound, lighting, video, and computer systems.

Many of the arresting pictures in this book attest to black churches that are coming of age as institutions of considerable influence, with their own built-in gymnasiums, day-care centers, educational facilities, computer laboratories, recording studios, and conference centers. Noteworthy also are a few African American megachurches with memberships in excess of ten thousand people and annual budgets over ten million dollars. Yet, the foundation for all of this is an uncanny sense of spiritual power that exudes on the Sabbath and is documented on every page of *Soul Sanctuary*.

Several years ago, when I was the guest preacher at a historic Baptist church in Washington, D.C.'s quaint Georgetown community, I was intrigued by a large number of European tourists who had taken seats in the rear of the sanctuary as part of their tour package in the nation's capital. These tourists were mostly from Germany and they had come to this small but venerable African American church to sample the richness of the black religious experience in a section of the city that was once entirely African American.

At one point in the service, an elderly black woman jumped to her feet and with arms flailing began walking back and forth in deep anguish, uttering a litany of moans and laments. Remarkably, the whole congregation spontaneously began singing as if on cue, providing some dark, mysterious comfort to this woman who, I soon learned, had only days earlier witnessed her twelve-year-old grandson shot to death on his way home from school. The mouths of the tourists fell open in awe, for they realized that they were privileged indeed to catch glimpses of the unique aesthetic that so often prevails in the soul sanctuary that epitomizes the black church worship experience.

The black church's impact on individual and community life, a life all too often threatened with crime, socioeconomic blight, and political disadvantage, has never been measured or fully appreciated. Over the years, the dynamics of the black church at worship have had a sustaining and healing impact on the lives of an important but often bedeviled American underclass. *Soul Sanctuary* shows us the faces of some of the people affected by this daily existence, as well as those who have escaped it.

Jason Miccolo Johnson's superb efforts in this treasure trove of photographs not only tell this important story of our spiritual heritage in these United States of America, but do so uniquely by letting everyone see the enduring strength of a too-often-neglected legacy. As one who has been deeply involved in the truth of Psalm 16:6 "Yea, I have a goodly heritage" (KJV), I share the author's view that *Soul Sanctuary* not only invites readers to join a continuing spiritual journey, but also encourages all Americans, particularly Christians, to celebrate this ecumenical cultural legacy, truly a "goodly heritage."

Usher Mack Paschal signals for one more person at Shiloh Baptist Church, Washington, D.C., 1998

Sister Lillie Patterson prepares the altar coverings for Sunday communion at
Hemingway Memorial AME Church, Chapel Oaks, Maryland, 1998

PREPARATION

This Is the Day Which the Lord Hath Made

This is the day which the Lord hath made; we will rejoice and be glad in it.
—PSALM 118:24 (KJV)

Early on Sunday morning, as the dawn stretches slowly across the horizon and while most are still blissfully asleep, a flurry of activity unfolds at black churches in preparation for the weekly worship service. Many of us probably just roll out of bed, dress in our Sunday best, and arrive at church without a thought as to what goes on before the fellowship begins.

Depending on the size of the church, it can take an army of one or one hundred to organize the various components of the traditional Sunday morning service well before the first note is played or the first prayer is uttered.

For Sunday school teachers, preparation often begins soon after the last class ends. Herb Rhedrick, a Sunday school and Bible study teacher at megasized Friendship Missionary Baptist Church in Charlotte, North Carolina, has, for more than a decade, diligently spent five to ten hours a week at home preparing lessons

ABOVE: Rev. Dr. Sally LaPoint (left) gets assistance with her collar from Deaconess Earlene Ladson before Brick Baptist Church's 150th anniversary celebration, St. Helena Island, South Carolina, 2005

for senior citizens and hundreds of young people. He pores over commentaries and religious literature, studying the historical background of the scripture lesson to understand the context in which the text was written.

"It's like preparing to preach a sermon," says Rhedrick, who is also an ordained minister. "But a sermon is a one-way message. In Sunday school you have to deal with questions about what you're teaching, so it's harder. . . . Preaching is for worship. The renewing of the mind comes from study and dialogue."

Rhedrick even takes the time to put together PowerPoint presentations for his classes. "That's what it's there for," he says of the high-tech wizardry. "It's created for the building of the kingdom."

Indeed, "kingdom building" begins early on Sunday mornings. Church caretakers, who often live nearby, emerge from the darkness to unlock doors and turn on sanctuary lights, air conditioners, or heat, anticipating the arrival of the pastor, deacons, and trustees for the morning service. In smaller churches, a deacon, trustee, or even the minister might be the first to arrive and unlock the doors. It's the first "opening of the doors of the church," long before the invitation to join the congregation is extended by the minister at the end of a sermon.

A young lady helps an elderly member to service at Metropolitan Baptist Church, Washington, D.C., 2004

Passenger vans, side panels emblazoned with the church's name and address, pull out of the parking lot and hit the streets en route to the homes of members who need a ride to church to get their "spiritual lift" for the week. Silas Lumpkins, a forty-year deacon at Morning Star Baptist Church in Cleveland, Ohio, is among those who drive in rain, sleet, or snow to pick up the faithful. As chairperson of Morning Star's Bus Ministry, he views driving as a way of showing his love for people. "It's a ministry because it's serving others," he says.

While drivers like Lumpkins are on the streets doing good works, ushers, stewards, and volunteers arrive promptly at church ready to perform a multitude of tasks that ensure the seamless flow of the service. Dressed in crisp, white, understated uniforms or sedate black suits, these dutiful souls stuff inserts into bulletins and restock pews with Bibles, hymnals, and offering envelopes before taking their places at entrances as saintly sentries to greet worshippers.

Many churches use stewardesses, trustees, or guilds to perform special functions within the sanctuary, such as maintaining the altar adornments. Traditional altar coverings change frequently throughout the month as well as seasonally, and attendees charged with their maintenance take great pride in the duty.

The altar is "an essential and integral part of the church's worship service," says

Nanette Harris, president of the Flower and Altar Guild at Cleveland's Morning Star Baptist Church. "Short of the minister and pulpit, as the congregation faces the front of the church, the focus of the church is the altar. It's what the people see when they first enter the church."

The kitchen of the fellowship hall also bustles with activity many Sunday mornings, as the church's culinary saints prepare favorite dishes like fried chicken, string beans, macaroni and cheese, potato salad, homemade rolls, and a crowd-pleasing peach cobbler for visiting guests expected at an afternoon worship service.

In larger congregations that broadcast or record their services, members of the Media Ministry arrive in the control booth to don headphones, check microphones, and organize the audio and video equipment that will capture the sights and sounds of the glorious next two—or three—hours. At megachurches, where thousands of different worshippers often attend one of three services throughout the day, parking attendants and security guards direct cars into vast parking areas. Some parking lots are so far away that golf carts are used to ferry members to the church.

There is artistry to the coordination of all of the functions necessary in preparing for services in the black church. While parishioners enter the sanctuary, stopping to greet neighbors and friends with smiles and hugs, plenty of activity is taking place behind the scenes. Choir members gather in dressing rooms to put on robes, check makeup, straighten neckties, and warm up their celestial voices before making that spirited and joyful processional through the sanctuary to the choir loft—marking the start of service. Musicians, too, take their places at pianos, organs, guitars, drums, and other instruments to accompany the choir.

Stewardesses Hilda Jackson (left) and Geraldine Williams dressing the altar at Bethel AME Church, Tallahassee, Florida, 2005

Many churches begin the morning worship with a devotional period of prayer and song, mostly led by the deacons, as parishioners pick up the tune of the hymn. Or a designated praise team leads this preparatory time of worship with uplifting songs and clapping—"I don't know what you come to do, but I come to praise His name," they might sing.

During this prayer, praise, and worship time, ministers may still be in their offices taking another look at sermon notes and scribbling a change or two, prior to joining fellow clergy in a circle of prayer before entering the pulpit. Then, as the ministers enter the sanctuary and everyone rises to their feet, a familiar call to worship can be heard in many black churches: "The Lord is in His holy temple, let all the earth keep silent before Him."

Sister Helen Hutchinson (left) and Sister Sarah Hardman of Wesley AME Church
arrive for early morning service, Houston, Texas, 2005

Morris Ruben Davis, Meeka Y. Robinson-Davis, and their children, Christiana and Christian,
pause for a picture before entering the sanctuary at West Angeles COGIC, Los Angeles, 2005

ABOVE: Sister Janice Warner (center) teaches the Youth Sunday school class at Wesley AME Church, Houston, Texas, 2005

RIGHT: Brother Michael Smith teaches the Adult Sunday school class in the sanctuary at Apostolic Church of God, Chicago, Illinois, 2005

Usher Quanda Finch chats with Karolynn Moore while folding bulletins
at Alfred Street Baptist Church, Alexandria, Virginia, 2005

Youth usher Vivica Brooks passes out fans to congregants during Deacons', Deaconesses', and
Evangelists' ordination service at Righteous Church of God, Washington, D.C., 2003

The Media Ministry readies the audio equipment and video cameras prior to
the start of worship services at Greater Mt. Calvary Holy Church, Washington, D.C., 2003

Rev. Desire P. Grogan plays the piano during dedication worship services
at the newly renovated Shiloh Baptist Church, Washington, D.C., 1998

Rev. Dr. James L. Netters, Sr., is helped into his robe in his study at
Mt. Vernon Baptist Church–Westwood, Memphis, Tennessee, 2005

Ministers join hands in prayer in the study of Rev. Dr. Frank M. Reid, III,
prior to service at Bethel AME Church, Baltimore, Maryland, 2004

Acolyte Domonique Price Morris lights a candle during the opening of the
worship services at Lane Tabernacle CME Church, St. Louis, Missouri, 2005

Deacon Darrell Spencer gives the devotional prayer at
New Northside MBC, St. Louis, Missouri, 2005

The Sanctuary Choir marches in during the processional
at Apostolic Church of God, Chicago, Illinois, 2005

Rev. Dr. Grainger Browning
(center), senior pastor of
Ebenezer AME Church,
kneels down in prayer upon
entering the pulpit.
Pastor Browning and
Co-Pastor Jo Ann Browning
(center, right) are in the
vanguard of husband/wife
pastorships in America.
Fort Washington,
Maryland, 1997

Soloist Shervonne Wells sings praises at Greater Mt. Calvary Holy Church, Washington, D.C., 2003

INSPIRATION

Make a Joyful Noise

Praise ye the Lord. Praise God in His sanctuary: praise Him in the firmament of His power. Praise Him for His mighty acts: praise Him according to His excellent greatness. Praise Him with the sound of the trumpet: praise Him with the psaltery and harp. Praise Him with the timbrel and dance: praise Him with stringed instruments and organs. Praise Him upon the loud cymbals: praise Him upon the high sounding cymbals. Let every thing that hath breath praise the Lord. Praise ye the Lord.
—PSALM 150 (KJV)

Praising the Lord in the sanctuary of a black church is unlike any other worship experience. It is lively. It is engaging. It is emotional. Through spirit-filled music, moving liturgical dance, and youthful foot-stomping step teams, African Americans praise God from the bottom of the pews to the top of the rafters.

When you step into most African American churches on Sunday morning, the sights and sounds are unforgettable: choir members sway in unison, piano chords joust

ABOVE: Dr. William Woods plays the pipe organ at Antioch Baptist Church, Cleveland, Ohio, 2005

with organ riffs, and drums keep time with bass guitars. Dancers dressed in multicolored, layered fabrics and long, white, flowing vestments lift holy hands to heaven as they leap through sanctified air. The congregants merge themselves with the spirit of the Lord as the choir's soloist, eyes closed and head thrown back, sings with religious abandon. The scene plays out the same across the country and across denominations—Baptist, Methodist, and Pentecostal alike—when black folk begin to worship.

Soloist Karin Cox of Grace Temple SDA Church in Fort Worth, Texas, hits a high note at Longview Heights SDA Church, Memphis, Tennessee, 2005

What would the black church be without its music? From heartfelt hymns and anointed anthems to soulful spirituals and rollicking rhythms of urban gospel, music moves the spirit and stirs the soul. It sets the stage for worship through both song and dance. "In one service you can experience three or four different genres of music," says Joyce Garrett, a choir director, pianist, and organist at the historic 203-year-old Alfred Street Baptist Church in Alexandria, Virginia. "Many people will choose a church because of the music. I've heard people say they can take poor preaching, but not poor music." Those sentiments don't minimize the importance of preaching. "The best churches have a great marriage of great preaching and great music," says Garrett.

The ministry of music is serious business in black churches. Musicians are often held in high esteem for their talent and ability to take worshippers with them on a spiritual journey through music. Energetic choir directors, with their animated facial expressions and flailing arms, spend long hours researching songs, arranging music, training voices, and coordinating selections with the pastor. Many congregations support several choirs within the church. They may be known as the Youth and Young Adult Choir, the Senior Choir, and the Mass Choir. Or perhaps they have more creative names like Voices of Triumph, the Choraleers, or the Gospel Inspirers. No matter what they're called, these singing saints, dressed in colorful robes bearing the choir's initials, dutifully take their places each Sunday in the choir loft.

Enslaved Africans brought their love of music from Africa to America, but they had to suppress their spirited style of worship when they attended their master's more sedate services. Slaves "let go and had church" in their own way at camp meetings, where they combined primitive drums with unabashed singing and dancing just like in the motherland. Their syncopated rhythms and impromptu singing resonate through modern-day worship services. Today, horns, guitars, synthesizers, and drums have joined the traditional piano and organ in the musical accompaniment, giving new meaning to "make a joyful noise unto the Lord."

In tiny churches amid the cotton fields of the Mississippi Delta, the woeful strains of a congregational hymn wafting out of a raised window of a Baptist church in the summer could make a passerby feel blessed in its hearing. After a devotional leader calls out the words of a hymn, such as "Father, I stretch my hands to thee," the congregation then sings those words in a signature call-and-response fashion. Some call it "lining a hymn." Others, especially churchgoers over age fifty from the South, call it "Dr. Watts," after Dr. Isaac Watts, a white, eighteenth-century English minister who believed preachers should write their own hymns. Somehow, Watts's name became synonymous with the slow, note-bending songs that are still staples in the devotional period at some rural and more traditional urban churches across America. Long ago, only the minister and perhaps a few others could read, thus the necessity for one person to call out not only the words of a song, but also its tempo—short, common, or long meter.

A member of the Birmingham SDA churches combined Male Chorus takes the lead at Longview Heights SDA Church, Memphis, Tennessee, 2005

However, new forms of praise and worship have taken root that are much more vibrant, spirited, and, some would argue, progressive. Visually, they are part sacred and part secular, yet biblically based. Some of the newer forms of worship expression gaining acceptance in black churches include praise step teams, praise mimes, and liturgical dancers. Praise step teams, especially popular with young people, are reminiscent of high school drill teams or sorority and fraternity step shows. Praise mimes perform to music, combining the best of pantomime and dance while using expressive, painted faces to convey their message. Liturgical dancers aspire to usher in the Holy Spirit through carefully choreographed movements of the entire body—especially the hands and arms—as an extension of the worship experience. Many of the liturgical dance groups are led by someone with previous training in one or several forms of artistic dance, including African, ballet, modern, or jazz. They use their talents to lift up the Lord. They do not dance for "entertainment," they insist, but for spiritual purposes.

But you don't have to dance like David, sing like an angel, or play a horn like Gabriel to praise the Lord. Whether musician, choir member, liturgical dancer, or visitor, each contributes to the rich inspirational tradition of the African American worship experience.

The children's choir of Shiloh Baptist Church, Washington, D.C., 1998

The children's handbell choir performs during ceremonial
groundbreaking services for Metropolitan Baptist Church, Largo, Maryland, 2004

Praise singers at Greater Mt. Calvary Holy Church, Washington, D.C., 2003

Singer Darius Twyman renders a solo during evening services on Palm Sunday
at the historic New Bethel Baptist Church, Detroit, Michigan, 2005

ABOVE: Members of the St. Francis de Sales Catholic Church liturgical dance team listen admiringly to the choir, New Orleans, Louisiana, 2005

LEFT: The choir director encourages the choir to raise their voices in the soulful sanctuary of St. Francis de Sales Catholic Church, New Orleans, Louisiana, 2005

ABOVE: Deaconess Marsha Jackson, a member of the St. Paul Voices Choir, lifts her arms in praise at St. Paul Baptist Church, Capitol Heights, Maryland, 2004

RIGHT: The Sons of Thunder men's choir of West Angeles COGIC, Los Angeles, California, 2005

44

A member of the praise team uses flags to usher in the spirit
of the Lord at Evangel Fellowship COGIC, Greensboro, North Carolina, 2005

Minister B. J. Daniels praises God through mime at
Greater Mt. Calvary Holy Church, Washington, D.C., 2003

OVERLEAF: Liturgical dancers leap into "sanctified air" during
the ceremonial groundbreaking service for the new
Metropolitan Baptist Church, Largo, Maryland, 2004

The step team adds energy to the services at
Alfred Street Baptist Church, Alexandria, Virginia, 2003

A young drummer enlivens the congregation with his musical talents during
the Women's Day program at True Light Church Baptist, Chicago, Illinois, 2005

LEFT: Minister of Music Dr. Christopher Hale conducts the band at the historic New Bethel Baptist Church, Detroit, Michigan, 2005

BELOW: A guest guitarist plays during the church anniversary celebration at Greater St. Peter MBC, Greenville, Mississippi, 2005

A worshipper is in reflective prayer at the altar at
Charles Street AME Church, Roxbury, Massachusetts, 2005

DEDICATION

Prayer, Praise, and Giving

*Be careful for nothing; but in every thing by prayer and supplication
with thanksgiving let your requests be made known unto God.*
—PHILIPPIANS 4:6 (KJV)

*Every man according as he purposeth in his heart, so let him give;
not grudgingly, or of necessity: for God loveth a cheerful giver.*
—2 CORINTHIANS 9:7 (KJV)

Prayer, praise, and giving—like the Father, Son, and Holy Spirit—are the trinity of a black church service. In fact, prayer and praise are acts of worship, which are all interwoven into a supreme act of dedication to the Holy Trinity. Prayer opens and closes each service and is ever-present throughout the sanctuary. Some of the types of prayers are those used to invoke the Holy Spirit to come into the service (the invocation), offertory prayers, healing prayers, prayers of thanksgiving, prayers of praise, and prayers of dedication. There are meditative prayers,

ABOVE: Rev. Joan King lifts her arms in praise during the annual Second Episcopal District
Conference held at Metropolitan AME Church, Washington, D.C., 1990

contemplative prayers, intercessory prayers (praying on behalf of another person), and corporate prayers (one person praying on behalf of many). Reasons to pray are limitless, and believers are exhorted to "Pray without ceasing" (1 Thessalonians 5:17).

With the words "Let us pray," heads are bowed and eyes are closed as music plays softly in the background. A blessed quietness descends as believers begin to talk to God silently or to listen as one person says a collective, impassioned prayer for congregants. The silence is broken periodically as believers utter confirmation of the prayer with "Yes, Lord!" and "Have mercy on us." Even when only one person is called upon to pray, everyone is spiritually connected.

Ushers stand tall as they join in the reading of the scripture at Mt. Vernon Baptist Church–Westwood, Memphis, Tennessee, 2005

Whether the prayers are directed to the Virgin Mary or various saints, as in the Catholic Church, or straight to the Almighty Himself, they are often petitions for help and guidance or pleas for forgiveness of sins. The faithful can speak to the Divine Creator while seated in the pews or kneeling at the altar. If overcome with emotion, some lie prostrate as they take their burdens to the Lord.

In the black church, few prayers are read from a book or recited—most are unrehearsed, personal expressions to the Lord that acknowledge the presence of a higher power. No request is too small or too large, be it for help with dwindling finances, gainful employment, divine guidance with wayward children, traveling mercies, deliverance from temptation, or supernatural healing.

Over the years, Ozia M. Sturgis, a longtime member of Morrisania Baptist Church in Bronx, New York—and a mother, grandmother, and great-grandmother—has prayed for many things and many people. "I pray because I find a solace praying, and my prayers are answered," she says. "There are things I prayed and the answers come so real. I pray because I am an obedient Christian."

Just as prayer is a real part of Sturgis's life, so is speaking in tongues for many believers. In some churches, such as Pentecostal or Apostolic, praying in tongues—speaking in a language unknown to those who cannot interpret it—is as common as reciting the Lord's Prayer. Praying or speaking in tongues is not practiced in most white churches, or even in many black churches, but it does add a distinctive element to any worship service. While it can be accepted or shunned in various congregations, praising God in tongues is a biblically acknowledged spiritual gift, according to some Bible scholars (as referenced in 1 Corinthians 12:10).

Praise is a participatory activity in the black church and believers are free to join in as they are moved to do so. Some clap their hands or raise them skyward to signify reverence or acknowledgment of the Holy Father. Others sit and sway with tear-stained eyes, whispering their thanks, while some shout in a frenzy, risking separation from hat, wig, or both. Still others spring to their feet and commence a "holy dance" in the aisles to glorify God as a song reaches a fever pitch. Often the sound of the organ pulls at one's heartstrings as drums summon something deeper. In the black church, praise comes in all octaves, but it is rarely quiet.

Praise can sometimes reach thunderous heights as congregants get caught up in the spirit. Multiple shouts of "Hallelujah!" and "Thank you, Jesus!" as the choir rises for one more chorus of a gospel favorite, can take a service to a new level or in an unexpected direction. Ushers and deacons with fans and tissue in hand often step to the aid of over-excited worshippers—those "slain in the spirit"—to help calm, revive, or prevent injury as "the spirit has its way."

Offertory time—the time to pass the collection plate—is a major part of any black worship service, a ritual that many embrace cheerfully.

The call to giving often comes as a minister, deacon, or steward quotes an offertory scripture from Malachi 3:10 in the Bible: "Bring ye all the tithes into the storehouse, that there may be meat in mine house, and prove me now herewith, saith the Lord of hosts, if I will not open you the windows of heaven, and pour you out a blessing, that there shall not be room enough to receive it."

Uniformed ushers—wearing the traditional all-white dresses or corporate-style blazers and suits—walk down the aisles with military precision, one gloved hand behind the back, the other gloved hand bearing silver or gold collection plates that they pass to congregants to place their offerings. Children proudly drop in quarters and dollar bills their parents have pressed into their hands as the choir renders some music to give by. In some churches, ushers direct congregants row by row toward baskets or tables at the front of the church while the choir might be singing, "You can't beat God's giving, no matter how hard you try."

A dramatic praise dance presentation is given during Metropolitan Baptist Church's Easter services held on the Washington Monument grounds, Washington, D.C., 1999

It is said that when the praises go up, the blessings come down. Prayer and praise are the foundation and purpose of every worship service in the black church. The act of giving tithes and offerings—the financial resources that God has given His people to meet their earthly needs—is a form of thanksgiving and praise in itself.

Together, prayer, praise, and giving are powerful personal expressions of love and dedication.

ABOVE: A family kneels in preparation for prayer during services at
St. Francis de Sales Catholic Church, New Orleans, Louisiana, 2005

LEFT: The congregation in prayer during the 169th church anniversary
at Second Baptist Church, Detroit, Michigan, 2005

Intercessory prayer being rendered by a deacon at Jake's Chapel, Greenville, Mississippi, 2005

A young boy follows the scripture at Alfred Street Baptist Church, Alexandria, Virginia, 2003

Dr. Robert G. Murray gives pastoral remarks at the
historic First Baptist Church, Norfolk, Virginia, 2005

The church announcements are read by Elizabeth Davis at
Charles Street AME Church, Roxbury, Massachusetts, 2005

"Passing of the peace": Congregants greet each other during the
welcoming of visitors at Alfred Street Baptist Church, Alexandria, Virginia, 2003

Hugs and greetings are exchanged at St. Francis de Sales
Catholic Church, New Orleans, Louisiana, 2005

Congregants join hands in praise at Bethel AME Church, Baltimore, Maryland, 2004

Bishop John Richard Bryant, presiding prelate of the Fifth Episcopal District
of the AME Church, kneels in prayer alongside New Shiloh Baptist Church pastor
Rev. Dr. Harold Carter, Sr., at Bethel AME Church, Baltimore, Maryland, 2004

A congregant follows the pastor's text in the Bible at
New Jerusalem Temple Bible Way Church, Washington, D.C., 2004

Rev. Dr. Larue F. Kidd blesses the tithes at
True Light Church Baptist, Chicago, Illinois, 2005

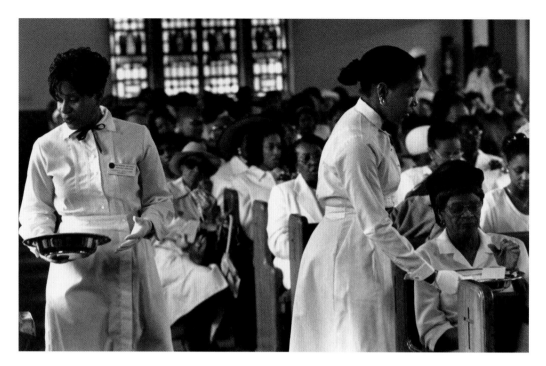

Ushers Laura Sullivan and Sandra Mauldin, dressed in traditional white uniforms, collect
the offerings at Ward Memorial AME Church, Washington, D.C., 1999

Joshua Hill (left) holds the basket as the Sunday offerings are deposited at
Ward Memorial AME Church, Washington, D.C., 2002

The stewards and trustees raise baskets for offertory prayer after taking up a special collection for community outreach programs at Ebenezer AME Church, Fort Washington, Maryland, 1997

ABOVE: Congregants kneel at the altar to pray at Pennsylvania Avenue AMEZ Church, Baltimore, Maryland, 2005

LEFT: Congregants gather closer toward the front of the sanctuary during altar call on Communion Sunday at Mt. Vernon Baptist Church—Westwood, Memphis, Tennessee, 2005

Rev. Dr. Gardner Taylor delivers an inspiring sermon at
St. Paul Baptist Church, Capitol Heights, Maryland, 2004

PROCLAMATION

The Preached Word

Preach the word; be instant in season, out of season; reprove, rebuke, exhort, with all longsuffering and doctrine. For the time will come when they will not endure sound doctrine; but after their own lusts shall they heap to themselves teachers, having itching ears.
——2 TIMOTHY 4:2–3 (KJV)

In many respects, the sermon—or the preached word—is the main event of the worship service. Those in the pews wait with anticipation for what those in the pulpit have to say. Ministers look to God to inspire them when preparing a sermon. It is an awesome responsibility to choose and dissect a scripture so that it is meaningful and applicable to the congregants' lives. Sermons aim to engage, inspire, and move people to action; whether it's to change to be more like the Supreme Being or to accept the most Holy One as the guiding force in their lives.

To fully appreciate the black worship experience is to understand the significance of the proclamation of the Word or "the Sermon." As it is today, the Sermon

ABOVE: Rev. John O. Peterson emphasizes the divine words of the Bible
in each of his sermons at Alfred Street Baptist Church, Alexandria, Virginia, 2003

in the early days of the black worship experience was the presentation of the immutable word of God. It spoke to the many issues and concerns faced by the congregation with a revelatory and resolute emphasis. The power of the proclamation gave hope to painfilled hearts and troubled minds. To hearts broken by the daily grind forged from a secular reality of racial discrimination and meanness, the proclaimed Word was challenged to address earthly woes and troubles. No matter what was going on in the lives of those who waited anxiously to worship, their sustaining selfdeclaration was "If I can just make it to church."

Rev. James W. Cox, pastor of Grace Temple SDA Church, preaches at Longview Heights SDA Church, Memphis, Tennessee, 2005

In a sense, it is the preacher's obligation to meet the expectation of those assembled that they will hear from heaven in a clear, passionate, and challenging oration. Indeed, the hearers desire the reaffirmation that God still sits high and looks low. They want to hear with conviction that the Lord Jesus Christ rose from the dead early one Sunday morning. Congregants look forward to the call and response between the pulpit and pew that asks, "Ain't He all right?" and affirms, "*Yeah!*"

The proclamation is the high point of the African American worship experience. Everything before the proclamation is in preparation for it, and everything after the proclamation is in response to it. It has been passed from one preaching generation to the next as a family art. For instance, the Reverend William C. Proctor, Jr., stated that his grandfather, the late Reverend James A. Proctor, told him that the recipe for effective preaching is a simple formula: "My granddaddy told me: Son, you start down low. Go slow. Aim high. Strike fire and sit down."

For sure, the drama, imagination, energy, and plain brilliance by which the black preacher draws allegiances, metaphors, analogies, humor, and other usable constructs to "Aim high and strike fire" are unparalleled in creativity and effect.

It is the presentation of the Word, the will, the way, the walk, the work, and the witness of God.

The Word has power and authority. If God said it, that settled it. The power of the declared Word gives meaning and purpose to the proclamation. When the black church gathers together it is understood that the Lord is in their midst and the congregation is subject to what the Lord said. In Psalms 119, David gives utterance to that which embraced the hearts of the worshippers when he said, "thy Word have I hid in mine heart that I might not sin against thee." Down through the years, the mysterious power and the glory of the preached Word has triggered inspiration in the hearts, minds, and souls of black parishioners.

The proclamation declares the will of God. It is understood that God's will is to be done, and that our will is to be subject to His will. The prayer of Jesus in the Garden of Gethsemane, submitting to the will of God His Father, has become an example and a reference for the saints in the black church of how to handle many challenges in life. There is knowledge that things did not just happen haphazardly, but rather the divine will of God directed all things.

The ways of God are not the ways of man. In Isaiah 55:8, the Word of the Lord declares, "For my thoughts are not your thoughts, neither are your ways my ways." This undeniable truth has been presented by way of proclamation and gives peace to our struggles. The walk of the brothers and the sisters gathered together in the black church is an emphasis of the proclamation. It is preached that we walk not by sight but by faith. We need to be in step with this Christian motif in order to keep our focus on the Word of God while we face obstacles and hindrances that challenge our faith.

When we think of the drive of the black community, we must think of the work of the black church, work that is the strength of the community. This is what makes the Bible more than a book of scripture verses; it is also a guide for living. The work of the Lord is the work of the black church. Luke 4:18–19 says, "The Spirit of the Lord is on me, because he has anointed me to preach the gospel to the poor; he hath sent me to heal the broken-hearted, to preach deliverance to the captives, and recovering of sight to the blind, to set at liberty them that are bruised, to preach the acceptable year of the Lord." This is the message of the proclamation.

Anita Carson and daughter Rasha Kilgore enjoy the sermon at Michigan Park Christian Church, Washington, D.C., 1995.

The proclamation is the presentation of the witness. Nothing is more convincing than the witness, and the preacher is that witness. When the Word, will, way, walk, work, and witness are presented through the proclamation, the power of the black church is released. Thus, the black community becomes emboldened with strength that brings about change for the better.

Finally, the invitation to new disciples, or "opening the doors of the church," is the affirmation of the proclamation. It is the time when those wishing to join the church or become candidates for baptism can walk down the aisles and profess their belief in God and their desire to be united in the body of Christ through the church. God is good all the time. And all the time God is good.

Rev. Evelyn Lee cites the text for her sermon, "A Mind Is a Terrible Thing to Waste,"
at First Baptist Church, Norfolk, Virginia, 2005

Parishioners share a Bible at St. Francis de Sales Catholic Church,
New Orleans, Louisiana, 2005

Bishop Willie James Ellis, Jr., preaches the morning service at
New Northside MBC, St. Louis, Missouri, 2005

Mrs. Lisha Morris, the First Lady of Lane Tabernacle CME Church,
enjoys a laugh during morning services, St. Louis, Missouri, 2005

A message of hope and joy is conveyed by guest speaker Elder Sherrilyn Williams,
the First Lady of World Overcomers Outreach Ministries, during the 68th Annual Women's Day
program at St. Stephen MBC, Memphis, Tennessee, 2005

Bishop T. D. Jakes, pastor of The Potter's House in Dallas, Texas,
is guest preacher at Metropolitan Baptist Church, Washington, D.C., 1999

Rev. C. W. Ray delivers a rousing sermon during his live Sunday morning
radio broadcast at Jake's Chapel, Greenville, Mississippi, 2005

Evangelist Vanessa Eshmon is overwhelmed by the Holy Spirit
during the morning worship service at Jake's Chapel, Greenville, Mississippi, 2005

ABOVE: Leona Anderson (left) and First Lady Marlaa Reid respond with raised arms to the preached Word at Bethel AME Church, Baltimore, Maryland, 2004

LEFT: Guest preacher Rev. Dr. Floyd Flake, pastor of The Greater Allen Cathedral of New York, kicks into another gear at Bethel AME Church, Baltimore, Maryland, 2004

TOP AND BOTTOM: Congregants react to the words of the guest preacher
at the former location of Reid Temple AME Church, Lanham, Maryland, 2003

Rev. Claude Alexander, Jr., senior pastor of the University Park Baptist Church in Charlotte, North Carolina, preaches during Greater Mt. Calvary Holy Church of America's International Convocation, Washington, D.C., 2003

ABOVE: Congregants listen closely to the words of Bishop Victor T. Curry in the overflow room at the former location of New Birth Baptist Church Cathedral of Faith International, Miami, Florida, 1998

RIGHT: Bishop Victor T. Curry preaches the second of his three Sunday services at New Birth Baptist Church, Miami, Florida, 1998

Rev. Gina M. Stewart, pastor of Christ MBC, moves the congregation
during her "Resurrection Sunday" message, Memphis, Tennessee, 2005

Apostle Betty P. Peebles, senior pastor and overseer, teaches from the scripture
Zechariah 2:8, Jericho City of Praise Church, Landover, Maryland, 2005

Rev. Dr. H. Beecher Hicks, Jr., challenges the congregation to "look where God has brought us
from" during his stirring resurrection homily at the ceremonial groundbreaking service for the
new Metropolitan Baptist Church, Largo, Maryland, 2004

ABOVE: Rev. E. V. Hill, pastor of Mount Zion MBC Church in Los Angeles, was the revival preacher for the tent service (shown at left), Glenarden, Maryland, 1998

LEFT: An old-fashioned tent revival held on the grounds of First Baptist Church of Glenarden hosted by a collaboration of local churches, Glenarden, Maryland, 1998

OPPOSITE AND ABOVE: A much sought-after revivalist, Rev. Jerry D. Black,
pastor of Beulah MBC in Decatur, Georgia, goes through the motions and emotions
of his sermon at Greater Mt. Moriah Baptist Church, Memphis, Tennessee, 2005

Bishop Alfonso Scott, pastor of Lively Stone Church of God, delivers the
Sunday night broadcast sermon, St. Louis, Missouri, 2005

Rev. H. Shirley Clanton, pastor of Lane Memorial CME Church, preaches
a communion Sunday message of "faith," Washington, D.C., 2004

Dr. Keith W. Reed, Sr., of Sharon Baptist Church, is one of many pastors using wireless
microphones during their sermons, Philadelphia, Pennsylvania, 2004

With the aid of large projection screens, Bishop G. E. Patterson, senior prelate of the
Church of God in Christ and pastor of Temple of Deliverance, can more easily be seen
by every member of his congregation, Memphis, Tennessee, 2005

Rev. Simmie Harvey shares divine words of wisdom with his congregation at
Mount Moriah MBC, New Orleans, Louisiana, 2005

Rev. Dr. Cardes H. Brown, Jr., delivers a thought-provoking sermon
at New Light MBC, Greensboro, North Carolina, 2005

A deacon gets the name of a new disciple during the invitation period at
Mt. Vernon Baptist Church–Westwood, Memphis, Tennessee, 2005

Pastor James L. Netters, Sr., comforts one of his congregants after she received
a special prayer at Mt. Vernon Baptist Church—Westwood, Memphis, Tennessee, 2005

ABOVE: A young man in a wheelchair leaves the altar after prayer at First AME Church, Los Angeles, California, 2005

RIGHT: Prayer throughout the sanctuary on Holy Communion Sunday at Big Bethel AME Church, Atlanta, Georgia, 2005

OVERLEAF: The first elected female bishop in the history of the AME church, Bishop Vashti Murphy McKenzie, preaches a soul-stirring sermon at Bethel AME Church, Baltimore, Maryland, 2005

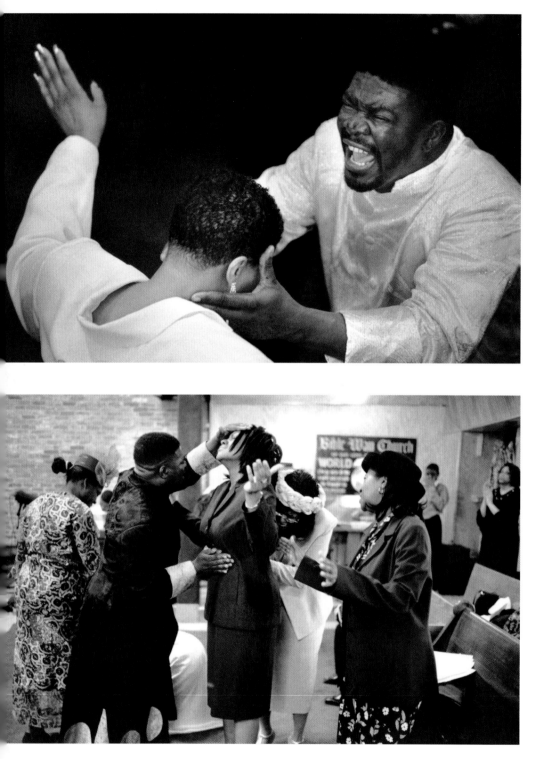

The energetic and powerful Bishop Abraham Mitchum, Sr., renders deliverance through the gift of "laying on of hands" at New Jerusalem Temple Bible Way Church, Washington, D.C., 2003

Rev. Edward Y. Jackson prepares to baptize a young convert at
Alfred Street Baptist Church, Alexandria, Virginia, 2003

CELEBRATION

Rites, Rituals, and Annual Days

And he took bread, and gave thanks, and brake it, and gave unto them,
saying, This is my body which is given for you; this do in remembrance of me.
—LUKE 22:19 (KJV)

I indeed baptize you with water unto repentance: but he that cometh
after me is mightier than I, whose shoes I am not worthy to bear:
he shall baptize you with the Holy Ghost, and with fire.
—MATTHEW 3:11 (KJV)

Worship within a black church is often described as a unique, invigorating, and soul-enriching experience that many relish each Sunday. But when those weekly gatherings are marked by a special occasion, the service is transformed into a spiritual celebration.

Much is celebrated in the black church, from the anniversaries of dedicated and faithful servants, such as the pastor and ushers; to annual Women's and Men's Days;

ABOVE: Four little girls gather on the steps after Easter services
at Ebenezer Baptist Church, Washington, D.C., 2000.

to the long-awaited marriage of a devoted member; to the "home-going" of a beloved soul. Rituals, such as the Holy Communion, which commemorates the death and resurrection of Jesus Christ, and the official welcome of new converts who are baptized and given the Right Hand of Fellowship, are also highlights to the worship experience.

Among the many other church rituals, baby dedications have become more popular in recent years. A precedent for them was set in biblical times when Hannah presented Samuel to God, and Mary and Joseph did the same with Jesus. Charlene and Ken Washington of Fort Washington, Maryland, followed suit and presented their first-born child, Jeremiah, for dedication when he was five months old.

Foot-washing ritual being conducted by Rev. Dr. Harry L. Seawright during Watch Night services at Union Bethel AME Church, Temple Hills, Maryland, 2004

"It was an opportunity for us to thank God for the gift of a child," says Charlene. "We both felt it was also the perfect opportunity for us to commit to God that we would train up Jeremiah to follow His commandments. It also gave us a peace of mind that he was blessed by God and under His eternal protection."

Along with the dedication of precious new life, churches dedicate new choir robes, new building additions, and new vehicles. Anything and everything that is used for God's glory and kingdom is dedicated to Him.

Many churches host a Homecoming Day, when former or relocated members and friends return to worship and enjoy a fellowship dinner at the church. And we cannot forget the three big holidays, when most sanctuaries overflow—Easter, Christmas, and Mother's Day—those times when "sometime saints" make their cameo appearances for the year.

The church is also host to celebratory rites of passage: birth, marriage, and death. Many Sundays find family and friends gathered together to witness the union of a blissful couple. When a beloved member dies, the funeral services or "home-going" held in the sanctuary celebrates their life and journey to a heavenly home.

Women's Day spotlights the dedicated sisters, often dressed in white or another designated color in a show of solidarity. This is one day that ladies will populate the pulpit and the speaker of the day is most likely a woman. On Men's Day, the brothers come together to stand up and be counted, with the sermon geared to their role at home and in the church. For Youth Day, the little ones nervously give their first public prayer or solo before anxious but proud parents, as they assume all of the leadership roles in the church for the day.

When it comes to religious rites of passage, baptism tops the list. For Christians, baptism signifies the death and resurrection of Jesus Christ, the washing away of sins and the beginning of a new life in Christ. The act is a form of initiation and a prerequisite for becoming a full-fledged church member.

Some denominations sprinkle new converts with water, while others require a full-body immersion in water. One by one, the young and the old are baptized "in the name of the Father, the Son, and the Holy Spirit" as onlookers applaud and thank God for another saved soul.

Before indoor baptism pools became a common part of church architecture, many new Christians were "dunked" or submerged outdoors in rivers, creeks, and ponds, especially in the South. Dressed in white gowns and head wraps (white is a symbol of purity and new birth), they often joyously sang a hymn like "Take Me to the Water," as they made their way to the water's edge. Today, some churches hold special waterside baptism services to remember and experience the ritual as their forefathers did long ago.

Sister Etherine Brown is honored with a plaque for her fifty years of dedicated service during the Annual Woman's Day program at Ward Memorial AME Church, Washington, D.C., 1999

Baptized believers have the right to participate in the sacrament of Holy Communion, also known as the Lord's Supper. At least once a month, they partake of the bread and wine in remembrance of Christ's suffering on Calvary's cross. As strands of "Let Us Break Bread Together" or "At the Cross" are played, deacons serve the "supper" of earthly elements—usually small wafers or crushed crackers (the bread, symbolizing Christ's body) and grape juice (the wine, symbolizing His blood) from gleaming silver or gold trays. And now, in a society that thrives on convenience, communion elements come in compact, ready-to-serve combos with a tiny wafer and a smidgen of wine bundled and sealed together.

One celebration held almost exclusively in black churches is Watch Night service, which traces its African American origin to December 31, 1862, the day before President Abraham Lincoln's Emancipation Proclamation was announced, freeing slaves in Confederate states. Although Watch Night had years earlier been celebrated in the Methodist church, African Americans made it their "Freedom's Eve" in honor of the New Year's Eve of 1862 when slaves gathered in churches to await verification that indeed they would soon be free. Watch Night is also a time to give thanks to God for making it through another year and to pray for a better year to come.

What better celebration than the celebration of freedom?

ABOVE, TOP: Rev. Dr. H. Beecher Hicks, Jr. (center), proves adept at "feeding the sheep" by grilling chicken during homecoming celebrations at Metropolitan Baptist Church, Washington, D.C., 1998

ABOVE, BOTTOM: Pastor Alonzo Jackson fills two carry-out containers with food during a 100th-anniversary homecoming celebration at Sunflower Chapel MBC, Murphy, Mississippi, 1998

RIGHT: A most cheerful server, Sister Marva Leach, prepares punch for the 169th church anniversary repast at Second Baptist Church, Detroit, Michigan, 2005

114

Father Victor Cohea blesses the sacraments during the Holy Eucharist at
St. Francis de Sales Catholic Church, New Orleans, Louisiana, 2005

TOP AND BOTTOM: Holy Communion: The ceremonial breaking of bread and pouring
of wine in remembrance of the broken body and blood of Christ sacrificed for all Christians,
Mt. Vernon Baptist Church–Westwood, Memphis, Tennessee, 2005

ABOVE: A congregant takes communion during services at Alfred Street Baptist Church, Alexandria, Virginia, 2004

LEFT: The men gather at the altar for a special prayer during Annual Men's Day services at Turner Memorial AME Church, Hyattsville, Maryland, 2004

A more than forty-year-old tradition of baptizing in the Chesapeake Bay at Taylor's Beach
is continued every third Sunday in August by Rev. T. Wright Morris (right),
pastor of Shiloh Baptist Church, Reedville, Virginia, 2003

The Sanctuary Choir sings as converts are baptized after the morning
worship service at Apostolic Church of God, Chicago, Illinois, 2005

ABOVE, TOP: Bishop S. C. Madison blesses a crowd of saints as they gather for a mass baptism during the United House of Prayer For All People's annual convocation, Charlotte, North Carolina, 1996

ABOVE, BOTTOM: Saints by the thousands gather from around the country for the annual mass baptism conducted by Bishop S. C. Madison in the swimming pool behind the United House of Prayer For All People, Charlotte, North Carolina, 1996

LEFT: Candidates from Shiloh Baptist Church waiting to be baptized stand quietly in early morning light along the shores of the Chesapeake Bay at Taylor's Beach, Reedville, Virginia, 2003

ABOVE: A mourner takes a picture of beloved musician Michael D. Hobbs during the home-going celebration held at the Greater St. Peter MBC, Greenville, Mississippi, 2005

RIGHT: The Rev. Dr. Jesse King eulogizes musician Michael D. Hobbs at Greater St. Peter MBC, Greenville, Mississippi, 2005

TOP AND BOTTOM: An exuberant bride, Tiffany Ellis, is united in matrimony to
Calvin O. Butts, IV, in the historic Abyssinian Baptist Church, officiated by its pastor
(Calvin's father), the Rev. Dr. Calvin O. Butts, III, Harlem, New York, 2004

First Lady Cassandra Kidd (Women's Day chairperson) and Pastor Larue F. Kidd
enjoy accolades from the congregation after a successful Annual Women's Day program
at True Light Church Baptist, Chicago, Illinois, 2005

Pastor's anniversary at Greater Mt. Sinai MBC is celebrated with gifts for
Rev. Dr. J. Edward Thompson and First Lady Marjorie V. Thompson for
thirty-seven years of dedicated service to the church, Chicago, Illinois, 2005

Shouts of "Hallelujah!" come from Maryland State Delegate Salima Siler Marriott
during a night service at Bethel AME Church, Baltimore, Maryland, 2004

Usher Kimberly McKinney passes out strips of palms during Palm Sunday services
at Ward Memorial AME Church, Washington, D.C., 1999

Members of the King Frederick Consistory #38 Prince Hall Masons conduct a special
Easter Sunrise Ceremony at Greater Middle Baptist Church, pastored by
Rev. Benjamin L. Hooks, Memphis, Tennessee, 2005

A sharply dressed young boy reads his Easter speech at
New Jerusalem Temple Bible Way Church, Washington, D.C., 2004

Children from Metropolitan Baptist Church use letters to announce Easter
on the Washington Monument grounds, Washington, D.C., 1999

ABOVE, TOP: On Resurrection Sunday on the grounds of the Washington Monument, a Metropolitan Baptist Church member portrays Jesus carrying the cross to Calvary, Washington, D.C., 1997

ABOVE, BOTTOM: A young congregant reenacts the crucifixion of Jesus at Christ MBC, Memphis, Tennessee, 2005

RIGHT: The Resurrection reenacted by members of Metropolitan Baptist Church, Washington, D.C., 1997

ABOVE: Pastor Otis Lockett, Sr., talks with a young girl during a baby dedication ceremony at Evangel Fellowship COGIC, Greensboro, North Carolina, 2005

LEFT: The men gather for a special service during the annual convocation of the Church of God in Christ at the historic Mason Temple, site of Dr. Martin Luther King, Jr.'s last speech, Memphis, Tennessee, 1997

Young children reenact the birth of Jesus in a Christmas Nativity play
at St. Augustine Roman Catholic Church, Washington, D.C., 2003

A parishioner carries the crucifix through the sanctuary at
St. Augustine Roman Catholic Church, Washington, D.C., 2003

ABOVE: Rev. Dr. Lee P. Washington greets worshippers at the end of Watch Night services at Reid Temple AME Church, Glenn Dale, Maryland, 2004

LEFT: Thousands of congregants stream into Watch Night services at the newly built Reid Temple AME Church, Glenn Dale, Maryland, 2004

An elderly couple departs Sunday morning services at
Metropolitan AME Church, Washington, D.C., 1997

BENEDICTION

Until We Meet Again

*The Lord bless thee, and keep thee: The Lord make his face
shine upon thee, and be gracious unto thee;
The Lord lift up his countenance upon thee, and give thee peace.*
—NUMBERS 6:24–26 (KJV)

Congregants stand and join in singing the closing hymn. The minister gives the benediction. The choir sings a threefold "Amen." The choir marches out of the sanctuary followed by the ministerial staff. All blend their voices in singing a familiar hymn: "God be with you till we meet again, by His counsel guide, uphold you. In his arms securely fold you. God be with you till we meet again. . . . Till we meet at Jesus' feet." The organ plays softly and the formal service is now over.

As the congregants exit the church they often greet each other, sometimes accompanied by a hug or a "holy" kiss on the cheek. Frequently, the pastor stands

ABOVE: Two congregants chat following worship services
at Central Baptist Church, Baltimore, Maryland, 2004

at the door and shakes hands and greets attendees as they depart. The pastor is very often praised for his sermon and many members indicate its particular significance for them. Visitors are greeted with extra enthusiasm and encouraged to come back again next Sunday.

After the service, the trustees retire to count the morning offerings. The deacons may confer about ministries to the sick and shut in. On Communion Sunday, deacons or deaconesses prepare to "carry communion" to persons unable to attend the worship service.

A church member prepares to leave Young Missionary Temple CME Church after morning services, Raleigh, North Carolina, 2005

Frequently, members of the congregation begin to move toward the basement or fellowship hall, where there is food prepared by the church cooks or volunteers. The children are often corralled and fed and then sent outside to play, with cautions about caring for Sunday clothes or shoes and with the customary admonition not to get into trouble. During the meal, people greet each other, discuss the pastor's sermon, or agree upon future schedules for programs within the church. Very often, various boards or interest groups hold meetings after the meal.

In smaller congregations, if meals are not served after the worship service, the pastor is typically invited with his or her spouse to lunch at a member's home. This is usually a festive occasion; the table is set with the best dishes, and flowers adorn its center. Church matters may be discussed, or the meal may be just an occasion marked by humor and good fellowship.

Gradually the members begin to disperse to their various homes, to brunch, or to visit the homes of others. The hope is that all who have worshipped depart now "to serve." Some will have meetings of church societies or committees during the week in continuation of the life of faith. One departs with the shared common prayer of benediction: *May the Lord watch between me and thee while we are absent, one from another.* And all the people say: *Amen, Amen, and Amen!* When all have departed, a deacon or trusted servant turns out the lights, locks the doors, and leaves the premises.

Members of Central Baptist Church wait on their rides after attending the
"100 Women in Hats" celebration, Baltimore, Maryland, 2004

ABOVE: After preaching, Bishop John Richard Bryant greets worshippers at his former church, Bethel AME Church, Baltimore, Maryland, 2004

LEFT: Members of Turner Memorial AME Church join hands for the benediction, Hyattsville, Maryland, 2004

The esteemed Rev. Dr. C. A. W. Clark, senior pastor of Good Street Baptist Church,
and one of the oldest active pastors in the country, gives a firm handshake
at the end of service, Dallas, Texas, 2005

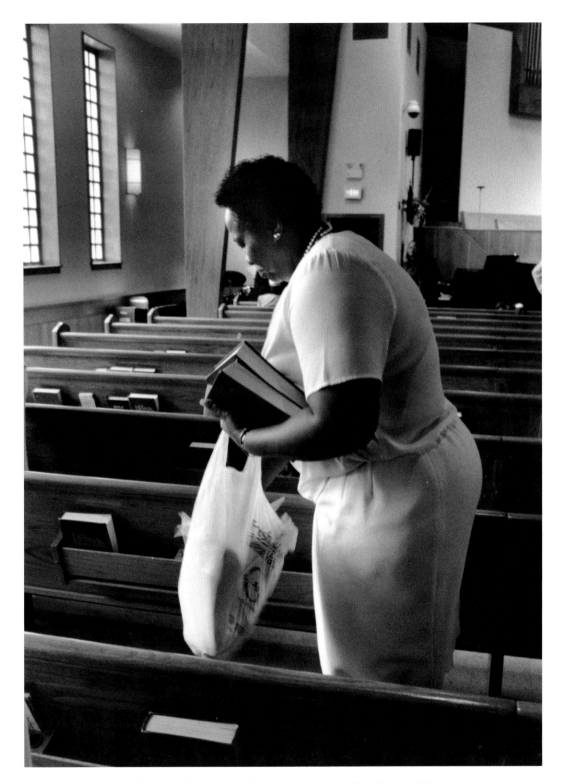

Usher Florence Davis gathers hymnals and items left in the pews following
the close of services at Alfred Street Baptist Church, Alexandria, Virginia, 2004

ABOVE: Karyll Josey of Greater Mt. Calvary Holy Church scans the selection of videotapes available at the end of morning service, Washington, D.C., 2003

LEFT: The Mother's Counsel of True Light Church Baptist enjoys the repast after the Annual Woman's Day program, Chicago, Illinois, 2005

151

ABOVE: Archbishop George A. Stallings, founder of the African American Catholic Congregation, greets parishioners after service as they depart Imani Temple on Capitol Hill, Washington, D.C., 1996

RIGHT: The last few members await their rides at Longview Heights SDA Church, Memphis, Tennessee, 2005

AFTERWORD
Bishop John Hurst Adams, retired

This photographic chronicle of worship in the black church has been aptly named *Soul Sanctuary*. It captures the tensions, ironies, and contradictions of black life in America, which are balanced and reconciled through the grace of God, and then celebrated in worship. They become a litany of the equilibrium we find in the "soul sanctuary."

Repression and Liberation
Powerlessness and Empowerment
Suffering and Healing
Exclusion and Inclusion
Limitations and Possibility
Pain and Pleasure
Control and Passion
Slavery and Freedom
Peoplehood and Personhood
History and Hope
Poverty of Wealth and Richness of Value
Adaptability and Stability
Bent Over and Looking Up
Glued to the Bottom and Reaching to the Top
Nobodyness and Somebodyness
Brokenness and Wholeness
Exploited and Forgiving
African and American

This is about what we have been through. This is about how we got over. This is about the grace of God. This is about the strength of the human spirit. This is about the capacity building of the faith. This is about occupying the future. When you worship in the black church in America, you experience both our history and our hope.

Our journey of several centuries in America is rich and strong in landmarks, definitions, language, theology, liturgy, celebration, and expression—now valued traditions that must be both preserved and cherished as never before.

Likewise, worship in the black church, while preserving these valued traditions, embraces openness to the new. Like creation, worship is a continuous process. This openness is what keeps the black church contemporary without being overcome by modernism. It is the special gift of reconciling various tensions, ironies, and contra-dictions in our life story that you see so clearly in our worship. We put a contem-porary celebration around a historic faith and theology that include all the variety of life experience, diversity, and even pluralism in the black community.

This gift of celebrating and reconciling is another large contribution of the black church in America, one that is needed more urgently now than ever, as our world becomes global and flatter at the same time—and more complex and smaller. The exponential explosion in science and technology still needs the guidance and governance of spiritual and moral determination. We know how to offer atone-ment to science and technology in the "soul sanctuary."

Thanks are due to Jason Miccolo Johnson for the marvelous pictorial history and story of worship in the black church. He has created a vivid portrait of that alternative culture, in which you see the equality and dignity of every person in the life and work and rituals of the black church, which always says "Yes" to us.

Members of the Stewardess Board sit together dressed in all-white suits at the Greater Allen Cathedral of New York, Jamaica, New York, 2000

EPILOGUE

A Sanctuary for My Soul!

Rev. Dr. H. Beecher Hicks, Jr.

sanctuary (sangk'chu.er'e), n. pl.-aries.
1. a sacred place; holy spot; place where sacred things are kept.
A church is a sanctuary . . .
—WORLD BOOK DICTIONARY

The introspective lens of Jason Miccolo Johnson has defied the dictionary definition of the term *sanctuary*. While the primary definition of the word is related to place and location, the images we have seen here more accurately define the word as sense, as feeling, as who we are in the eyes of others and what we are becoming in the eye of the One who is Wholly Other. Sanctuary is not place; it is people. Sanctuary is more than space; sanctuary is a state of being and becoming.

Sanctuary is more than a church building. It is more accurately that gathering place where prayers are brought with trembling hands and quivering tongues.

Sanctuary is that assortment of styles, dressed to the nines, wigs pulled, hair fried, knowing that as we worship we are standing in the presence of that which we can never know nor adequately define.

Sanctuary is that secret shelter David described, where one gains the privilege of hiding out "under the shadow of the Almighty."

Sanctuary invites the homeless in and assures them that they are as welcome in the first pew as they are in the last.

Sanctuary places no value on poverty or wealth, those tragic illusions of social distinction that divide us and never unite us.

Sanctuary is a "just as you are" situation—what we wear is what we have, but we always come together in our "Sunday-go-to-meetin'" clothes.

Sanctuary is a moment when sins are confessed and forgiven, when broken relationships are renewed to start all over again, when weary and wounded travelers are able to touch the Hem of that Garment we believe brings healing and new life.

A beautiful stained-glass window given by the people of Wales
adorns the balcony of the historic Sixteenth Street Baptist Church
(site of the fatal 1963 bombing), Birmingham, Alabama, 1996

Sanctuary opens the ear to hear the Word, the Gospel, the Good News, the Word we need at the right time; the Word that brings salvation on its wings.

You can call sanctuary anything—Baptist, Methodist, Episcopalian, Church of God in Christ or Community this or that—what you call it is not as important as what you experience: family time, "holy hugs," fresh waters for baptism, broken bread, flowing wine, swaying choirs, silver-tongued preachers, a moment to "get your step in," hold your head back and holla, a "fellowship, a joy divine."

If sanctuary is only a place, however, the place may disappear.

If sanctuary is only a building, the building may decay and disappear with the passage of time.

If sanctuary is merely a "church," church may not always be what I need.

It is this and more. Sanctuary is where my soul finds peace, where my soul connects to its Savior, where my spirit finds contentment, where my heart is at rest, where the pains and sorrows of this world disappear if only for a moment. I'm glad I found it. Jason Miccolo Johnson has helped me to see it. That *Soul Sanctuary*—it's really my home. I don't know about you, but I'm going back. . . .

ACKNOWLEDGMENTS

I wish to first thank Gordon Parks for providing *The Learning Tree*, the fruit of which I have gratefully picked. As a direct result of Gordon's trailblazing accomplishments and ceaseless creative energy, I am both inspired and prepared to give birth to the first of many visual progenies. I think the firstborn is always celebrated more for its anticipated arrival than for its actual birth. Thank you to Manie Barron, my agent and "birthing coach," for getting the book into capable hands. As with childbirth, I'm told, there is a certain degree of pain that comes with a labor of love. *Soul Sanctuary* owes its delivery to the midwife team of publisher Jill Cohen, an accomplished professional with a firm handshake, gentle smile, and proven business acumen, and Michael L. Sand, a calming and focused spirit who is the consummate editorial director. Hats off to the dedicated team at Bulfinch Press. I am equally delighted with the way book designer Laura Lindgren "laid hands" on the pages of *Soul Sanctuary*.

I wish to thank journalist and friend Barbranda Lumpkins Walls for writing four of the six essays. Barbara's flair for writing in the authentic voice of the black church was invaluable. Special thanks to Dr. Cain Hope Felder for making time on a tight schedule to write the introduction, and to Bishop John Hurst Adams for bringing an owl's wisdom and an eagle's perspective to the afterword. To Rev. Cardes H. Brown, Jr., author of the "Proclamation" essay, and Dr. Lawrence N. Jones, former dean of the Howard University School of Divinity and author of the "Benediction" essay, my sincere thanks for your poignant prose and steadfast support. Special thanks are due Rev. Dr. H. Beecher Hicks, Jr., for writing the epilogue. You were one of the first to believe in the book ten years ago.

To my personal success and sanity barometers, James A. Carter and William Proctor, Jr., thanks for listening, sharing, understanding, and being there at every step of the way. Mr. Carter, thanks for being the epitome of a best friend, for all the "harvest time" moments, and for allowing me to borrow your *monster vision plus massive action equals mega success* formula. "Mr. President" (Proctor), thanks for your writing, wisdom, hospitality, and for all of your "executive orders."

Along this road to publication are many persons who gave me advice, food, shelter, finances, and resources, but most of all, their friendship. Special thanks are in order to the following: Marvin Morgan, my lifelong friend, for always being there; David Wright, for getting me started in photography; George Hunt and Davis Penn, my first art teachers; Ernest C. Withers, my beloved friend, father figure, and mentor for making key contacts on my behalf in Memphis; Charles Burton, my special Republican friend for opening your home and your world to me; Rev. John O. Peterson, for permitting me to document Alfred Street Baptist Church's bicentennial year and later for extending the right hand of fellowship; Thomas and Marsha Blanton, for your unwavering moral support; Lisa Crump Williams, for sharing spiritual insights, particularly during the summer of 2004; Angela Terrell Heath for assistance with the news releases; Bob Black and Servelure McMath, for hosting me in Chicago; Elaine Robinson, for your loyalty and empowering words of encouragement; Keith Matthews and Alvin Kendall for hosting me in Houston and Atlanta respectively; Herman Rankins, for continuing to give musically and inspirationally; Tommie Johnson, my eldest brother, for taking care of me in St. Louis as always; photographers Maurice Meredith and Wiley Price, for giving generously of their time and contacts; Tony Decaneas and Miss Velma Dupont, for the southern hospitality shown me in Boston; and Jim Thorns for taking good care of me in New Orleans.

I imagine that in every major endeavor, one reaches a point where creative gas is about to run out and you arrive at the intersection of Required Avenue and Necessary Street. "After you have done all that is required," says motivational speaker Les Brown, "then you must do what is necessary." To Dr. Stella L. Hargett, I offer my sincere gratitude to you for helping me to do what was necessary, and for your assistance in editing on deadline. A special thanks to Wayne Rainey for the countless hours you spent charting the course with your visionary graphic design of the preliminary layout, and to Dudley Brooks for your daring eye and rapid-fire picture editing.

Special thanks to Harlee Little for always coming through with time-saving advice and technical support just when I needed it most. I also give a sincere thank-you to Chrome, Inc., and its very fine staff for not only the quality lab work, but also for the patient support and encouragement given me by the best customer service team on the East Coast.

To Shirl Spicer, my chief researcher, travel agent, proofreader, executive assistant, and number-one cheerleader, I give my deepest appreciation.

I'd like to lift up the names of Bishop Alfred A. Owens, Jr.; Rev. William Porter; Dr. Frank M. Reid III; Rev. Dr. Barbara Reynolds; Bishop A. J. Richardson; Rev. Robert L. Thomas, Jr.; Dr. A. C. D. Vaughn; and Rev. Jonathan Weaver for generously sharing knowledge and church contacts.

And finally, my heartfelt appreciation goes to the more than two hundred pastors who graciously blessed me with the opportunity to photograph their churches and their worship services. My only regret is that I couldn't include every church in the book. Please note that due to space limitations, many churches are not shown in the book; they may be seen in the traveling exhibition and on my Web site, www.soulsanctuarybook.com. God bless you all.

LIST OF CHURCHES

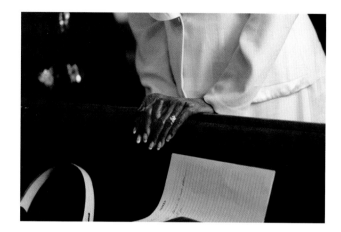

BULFINCH PRESS
Time Warner Book Group
1271 Avenue of the Americas, New York, NY 10020
Visit our Web site at www.bulfinchpress.com

First Edition: April 2006

ISBN 0-8212-5790-0
Library of Congress Control Number 2005930085

For information regarding sales to corporations, organizations, mail-order catalogs, premiums, and other
nonbook retailers and wholesalers, contact: Special Markets Department, Time Warner Book Group,
1271 Avenue of the Americas, 12th floor, New York, NY 10020-1393, Tel: 1-800-222-6747

ABOVE: An elderly woman grips the back of a pew as she stands at Payne Cathedral of Faith AME Church,
Houston, Texas, 2005; PAGE 1: Evangelist Vanessa Eshmon feels the spirit at Jake's Chapel, Greenville, Missis-
sippi, 2005; PAGES 2–3: The invitation to Christian discipleship is given during services at Alfred Street Baptist
Church, Alexandria, Virginia, 2003; PAGE 4: Tambourines at Wesley AME Church, Houston, Texas, 2005

Design by Laura Lindgren

PRINTED IN SINGAPORE